R. G. Morgan

The Tale of Rhea & Groat

Bumblebee
Books

A CIP catalogue record for this title is available from the British Library.

ISBN: 978-1-83934-841-9

Bumblebee Books is an imprint of
Olympia Publishers.

First Published in 2023

Bumblebee Books
Tallis House
2 Tallis Street
London
EC4Y 0AB

Printed in Great Britain

Dedication

I dedicate this book with love to my brother Carlos Arturo.

Also to my two beautiful children, Charlie & Aurora,

who inspire me every day.

ONE EARLY MORNING, Rhea was digging for carrots when
an alligator appeared out of the pond behind her.

"Good morning," the alligator cheerfully said, his mouth wide
open. "My name is Groat."

Groat saw no reaction to his friendly greeting.
"Good morning," repeated Groat, coming a little closer to the
white-tailed jackrabbit who stood with
her back to him.

"GOOD MORNING!" said Groat, a little
louder this time.

Suddenly, one of Rhea's long ears stood up, and she quickly
turned around. She saw a large, celery-green reptile staring at
her through thick glasses and
a wide-open mouth.

Startled, Rhea dashed inside her treehouse and
closed the door, leaving her basket full of
carrots behind on the ground.

I could have been eaten alive, thought Rhea.

Her heart was racing really fast. From the window of her door,
she could see that Groat had returned to the pond and slowly
headed back into the water.

With a flick of his giant tail, he turned around to look at Rhea.
He had two big eyes behind his big thick glasses,
a toothy smile, and a big fat belly.

His belly is three times larger than the rest of his body, thought Rhea.
"You scared me to death!" she screamed
through her glass window.

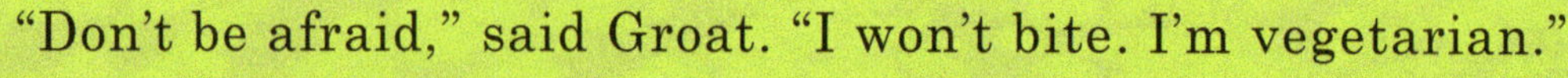

"Don't be afraid," said Groat. "I won't bite. I'm vegetarian."

LATER THAT DAY, all Rhea could think about
was that large alligator with eyeglasses.
What a strange fellow, she thought.

She brought out her gardening tools to start a new patch of
plum tomatoes, peppermint, and tart cherries.

"I see you're starting a new patch," said a slow-moving
chameleon as it made its way down from
a nearby tree. "How goes it, Ree?"

"Oh my! You scared me!" said Rhea, happy to see her good
friend Gayle. "I would have completely missed you
if you hadn't changed into a different color."

"Yeah, I know," said Gayle. "I try to blend in, but for you,
I don't mind getting noticed."

"You are not going to believe who I met this morning," said Rhea, adjusting her pink bow and looking around suspiciously. "I met a friendly alligator who wears eyeglasses."

"Ree, are you talking about Groat?" asked Gayle. "No, not a talking goat—an alligator," said Rhea.

"Yeah, I know him," said Gayle. "His name is Groat, and he's harmless. In fact, he likes to hang out with Remy, the ancient albino giant tortoise."

LATER IN THE EVENING, Groat was cooling off his long tail at his favorite spot atop a rock at the end of the pond.

All Groat could think about was the jackrabbit farmer he had met that morning—and her delicious carrots.

"You seem lost in thought, amigo," said a giant tortoise, who slowly walked toward Groat.

"Hey Remy!" said Groat, looking up while adjusting his eyeglasses. "Good to see you again, buddy."

"How did you know it was me?" asked Remy.

"I could hear you limping from a mile away," said Groat, continuing to dip his tail in the water. "How's your gout?"

"It's acting up again..." said Remy, soaking his swollen front leg in the cool water. "... but I'll live."

"You know, I read about a remedy that involves eating tart cherries," said Groat, sounding concerned. "It can help reduce the swelling in your leg."

"I'm willing to try anything at this point," said Remy, feeling a little tired. Groat decided to come out of the water to tell Remy about the jackrabbit he met that morning.

"This morning, on the other side of the pond, I met this jackrabbit who likes to farm, and—"

"I see you've met Rhea," interrupted Remy.
"She's always busy digging carrots or planting something.
But she likes to keep to herself."

"I've never seen her before," said Groat. "But then, I think my
eyesight is getting worse, so I blame my eyeglasses."

"No, I think what you need is to eat more carrots," said Remy,
matter-of-factly. "I hear it helps improve vision."

"Imagine that," said Groat. "Good to know."

THE NEXT DAY, Rhea was busy watering her carrots,
peppermint shrubs, and tart cherries. This time, Rhea clearly
saw Groat coming out of the water and quickly ran toward
the treehouse with her basket of carrots.

"Good morning," said Groat, in a friendlier tone.
"Please come back. Don't be afraid."
From where Rhea was standing by the doorway,
she could see that Groat was at the edge of the pond.

"What do you want?" asked Rhea, surprised to see the friendly
reptile with large eyeglasses again. "My name is Groat.
I am an alligator."

Rhea took a few steps back, ready to
climb up to her treehouse.

"Are those carrots you're holding?" asked Groat, lifting his
long nose in the air and fascinated by the aroma. "I can barely
see them, but I can smell them from here."

"Yes," said Rhea. "Would you like to … eat one?"
"Oh yes!" replied Groat, twitching his
eyelids with excitement.

"Hmm, I thought alligators didn't eat vegetables," Rhea replied
with a puzzled look.

"Oh no, I love all kinds of vegetables!" said Groat joyfully.
"I'm so hungry right now that I could eat a horse—I mean, a
horseradish! And carrots are my favorite!"

From a safe distance, Rhea threw a single carrot.
"Here, catch!"

Groat caught the carrot midair with a magnificent display of rolling acrobatics, swallowed it in one gulp, and then splashed down into the pond, with his big belly.

"Yum! Tasty! This carrot is delish!" said Groat.
"What are those things resting on top of your nose?" asked Rhea, fascinated by this big, friendly, vegetarian alligator.

"Oh, these?" said Groat, looking down with crossed eyes while adjusting his spectacles. "They're called *pince-nez*, and they help me see better. Otherwise, everything is blurry. I'm a voracious eater—I mean reader."

"I see. What is ... pawns-nay?" asked Rhea, trying to pronounce it.

"Well, basically, they are glasses that pinch onto your nose," explained Groat. "What is that pink thing in your ear?"

Rhea quickly adjusted her pink bow to cover her hearing aid.

"I can't hear very well," she said, pointing to her ears.
"I wear a special device to help me hear better.
And this pink bow conceals it for me."

"I hear ya," said Groat, with a wink.

"Forgive me," said Rhea, "but I must go now."
"Please don't go. What is your name?"
asked Groat, gingerly.

"I don't see very well," he continued, squinting and moving alittle closer to Rhea. "What are you?"

"My name is ... Rhea," she replied, nervously.

"Nice to meet you, Rhea," said Groat. "You have pretty hair."
"Yes, I am a prairie hare," said Rhea, "a jackrabbit."

EARLY THE NEXT MORNING, Gayle was rinsing tart cherries with some pond water. From the corner of her eye, she saw a lovebug crawling down a tree branch and swiftly snatched it with her long tongue.

Too bad I can't tell what this tastes like, said Gayle to herself as she swallowed it.

"Hello there, Gayle!" said Groat, who came out of the pond and approached her slowly. "Groat, yesterday you frightened my friend Rhea," said Gayle, sounding a little annoyed. "You scared her to death!"

"Oh, I know. I didn't mean to, Gayle," said Groat apologetically. "Sometimes, I just let my voracious hunger get the best of me."

"What's eating you?" said Gayle, jokingly. "Oh, nothing.
I just wanted to say hello."

Groat noticed Gayle had a basket full of tart cherries and a pot
of boiling water next to a tree.

"I see you are boiling water," observed Groat.
"Are you making soup?"

"No, I'm preparing some peppermint tea," replied Gayle,
closing the lid on the kettle.

"Rhea says peppermint leaves can help heal
my taste buds."

"Cool. It smells wonderful," said Groat. Adjusting his
eyeglasses, he got a little closer and added,
"Are those ... tart cherries?"

"Indeed! My friend Rhea gave them to me," said Gayle. "Nice.
Could you spare a few, please?" asked Groat.

"I'd love to give them to my friend Remy. He suffers from gout,
and this fruit may be a good remedy for him."

"Of course, you can! Here, have the whole basket," said Gayle
enthusiastically. "I hope Remy gets well after having these
delicious tart cherries..."

MANY WEEKS LATER, Groat, Remy, and Gayle
visited Rhea just before sundown. They were thankful for
Rhea's harvest of fruits and vegetables. "My gout is gone," said
Remy. "Thank you for the tart cherries, Rhea!"

"I can taste everything now," said Gayle. "Thank you for the
peppermint leaves, Ree!"

"I can see better," said Groat, adjusting his eyeglasses. "Those
carrots have been an eye-opener. Thank you, Rhea!"

"You are most welcome," said Rhea, blushing. "Thank you.
Thank you. Thank you for the kudos!"

LITTLE AURORA HAD BEEN PLAYING with her tea set and all her stuffed animals in her family's front-yard vegetable garden well into the evening.

"Sweetie honey," her mother called out, "come inside and have dinner with us."

"Ok, mommy, I'm coming," Aurora replied, shaking the dirt off her dungarees.

She stood up and looked down at her toys on the ground. "I wonder what adventures you'll have tomorrow," she said, leaving the stuffed rabbit, alligator, chameleon, and turtle in the vegetable garden as the spring sun set.

About the Author

When he is not writing in his favorite chair and typewriter, Rene spends most of his time reading, cooking, and playing chess - and not necessarily in that order. Rene lives in Fort Lauderdale, Florida with his wife and their two children.